Stay Out Of Court
And
Stay In Ministry

Clarance E. Hagglund
and
Britton D. Weimer

CSS Publishing Company, Inc., Lima, Ohio

STAY OUT OF COURT AND STAY IN MINISTRY

Copyright © 1998 by
CSS Publishing Company, Inc.
Lima, Ohio

All rights reserved. No part of this publication may be reproduced in any manner whatsoever without the prior permission of the publisher, except in the case of brief quotations embodied in critical articles and reviews. Inquiries should be addressed to: Permissions, CSS Publishing Company, Inc., P.O. Box 4503, Lima, Ohio 45802-4503.

Library of Congress Cataloging-in-Publication Data

Hagglund, Clarance E.
    Stay out of court and stay in ministry / Clarance E. Hagglund and Britton D. Weimer.
      p.   cm.
    ISBN 0-7880-1185-5 (pbk.)
    1. Clergy—Malpractice—United States. I. Weimer, Britton D., 1959- . II. Title.
KF4868.C44H34   1998
344.73'096—dc21   97-39507
                                                                         CIP

ISBN 0-7880-1185-5   PRINTED IN U.S.A.

About The Authors

Clarance E. Hagglund, J.D., is a litigation attorney practicing primarily in insurance coverage, professional liability, and other complex commercial litigation, trial and appellate. He is a Civil Trial Specialist certified by the National Board of Trial Advocacy, a National Board of Trial Advocacy Director, a Diplomate with the American Board of Professional Liability Attorneys, a Fellow with the International Society of Barristers, and a member of the Professional Liability Section of the Federation of Insurance and Corporate Counsel. Mr. Hagglund is the senior partner of Hagglund, Weimer & Speidel in Minneapolis, Minnesota. He is a member of The Basilica of St. Mary, Minneapolis.

Britton D. Weimer, J.D., is a litigation attorney practicing primarily in insurance and commercial litigation, trial and appellate. He is licensed to practice law in Texas, Wisconsin, Minnesota, and the Eighth Circuit Court of Appeals. Mr. Weimer is the author of articles published in the *Federation of Insurance and Corporate Counsel Quarterly*, the *Real Estate Law Journal*, the *International Society of Barristers Quarterly*, the *Hofstra Property Law Journal*, and the *Banking Law Journal*. Mr. Weimer is a partner at Hagglund, Weimer & Speidel. He is a member of Woodridge Church in Orono, Minnesota.

Mr. Hagglund and Mr. Weimer have co-authored several claims-prevention books for non-attorneys, including *Stay Out of Court and Stay in Business* (2nd ed., Common Law Publishing, 1996).

Acknowledgments

The authors appreciate the assistance of Reverend Carl Buettemeier of Newport Lutheran Church. They also are grateful to Kim Smiley's careful work typing and proofreading the manuscript.

Table Of Contents

Introduction	7
Chapter 1 Accidents And Injuries	9
Chapter 2 Clergy Malpractice	17
Chapter 3 Sex Abuse	25
Chapter 4 Employment Disputes	31
Chapter 5 Property Disputes	39
Chapter 6 Liability Insurance Policies	47
Chapter 7 Arbitration And Mediation	53
Endnotes	59

Introduction

Stay In Ministry is written to help pastors prevent costly and career-ending lawsuits. It sets forth the most common legal claims asserted against religious organizations, and the defenses churches have successfully raised. Finally, the book provides simple claims-prevention procedures that any church can use to dramatically reduce the risk of litigation.

Stay In Ministry is not primarily a book of theory. We describe real-life legal claims against churches and analyze the outcomes, pro or con. We focus on the claims most frequently asserted against churches. Some of the trends defy conventional wisdom. For example, there are few suits for clergy malpractice, but many successful suits for slippery sidewalks!

However, we do not avoid contemporary concerns. In particular, the book addresses the tragic increases in sex-abuse claims against churches. Although little can be done to insulate individual ministers who engage in such practices, much can be done to reduce false claims and to protect churches and denominations.

Stay In Ministry also addresses the limits courts place on themselves under the First Amendment of the Constitution. Pastors often see the "negative" side of the First Amendment, when it is used to restrict religious influence in government activities. However, the "positive" side of the First Amendment frequently shows up in lawsuits against churches. The courts routinely refrain from considering legal claims which require evaluation of church doctrine and practice.

The book describes the commonly available liability insurance policies which protect against many of the lawsuits described in the book. Sadly, an entire church can be financially ruined by a legal claim that would have been covered by an inexpensive insurance policy.

Finally, *Stay In Ministry* discusses two alternatives to lawsuits — arbitration and mediation. Both procedures are encouraged by the courts and are well suited to resolving most of the legal conflicts your church will face.

Chapter 1

Accidents And Injuries

Unless your state has charitable immunity, your church faces legal liability for the same bodily injuries as would a for-profit business.

Slip And Fall

Churches are frequently found liable for the injuries of a person who slips and falls on its property. For example, a volunteer youth instructor leaving a Montana church slipped on a sloped, icy sidewalk. She landed on her head and neck and damaged her spine. The instructor sued the church for failing to put salt on the ice and failing to put handrails on the sloped sidewalk. The jury awarded her $402,000.[1]

Similarly, a stranded Indiana motorist slipped on loose parsonage steps while looking for help. He sued the church for his injuries. The church argued that it had no duty to warn non-parishioners. The court rejected this defense, holding that the loose steps were not obvious, and that the church had a duty to warn all people of hidden dangers.[2]

However, there is normally no duty to warn of an open and obvious danger. Thus, a North Carolina bingo player was unsuccessful in a suit for injuries when she fell on a wet floor. The court held the danger was obvious, even if she had not noticed the water.[3]

Likewise, a church is not required to anticipate every possible risk that a person will slip and fall on its property. An Ohio woman was killed when she slipped and fell on a church's interior ramp. The ramp was slippery from water tracked in by the woman and other attenders. The woman's estate claimed the church should have put non-slip materials on the ramp. However, the church had provided mats immediately inside the entryway. The court dismissed the negligence claim against the church, because it had used the reasonable care expected of a business owner. "It is not necessary for a property owner to place mats or signs in every conceivable place an accident could occur when its patrons are on notice of the hazards of inclement weather."[4]

Attractive Nuisance

The doctrine of "attractive nuisance" means that a property owner is liable when neighborhood children are drawn to "attractive" hazards on the property. For example, a five-year-old Colorado child rode his bicycle down the church's curved wheelchair ramp and was struck by a car when he emerged onto the street. His family sued the church, claiming that the church knew neighborhood children rode their bicycles on the ramp but failed to install a fence or post warning signs. The church argued that the child had assumed the risk of injury. The court rejected this defense. "A child who has not reached his seventh birthday is incapable of knowing and voluntarily assuming a risk of harm."[5]

Similarly, a New York church was subject to suit when two teenagers climbed onto a tent erected for the church bazaar and fell from its roof. The court noted that the pastor knew children were playing near the tent, and that he had warned the two teenagers to stay away from the tent. Because of this knowledge, combined with the "well-known propensities" of children to "climb about and play," the church had a duty to erect a fence or take other security precautions.[6]

However, the attractive nuisance doctrine does not apply if the youth "appreciated" the danger. For example, an 11-year-old boy raced his bicycle down a church driveway into a city street, was hit by a car, and died from his injuries. His family's wrongful-death suit claimed that the church was responsible for the dangerous condition. The court rejected the family's argument and dismissed the suit, holding that the child knew of and understood the danger. "The possessor [of land] is not subject to liability to a child who in fact discovers the condition and appreciates the full risk involved, but nonetheless, chooses to encounter it out of recklessness or bravado."[7]

Criminal Acts On Property

Your church can be sued for negligently hiring a dangerous employee. In Virginia, a church employee sexually assaulted a member of the church, who brought suit against the church and pastor. The court held the church could be liable for failing to discover the employee's prior conviction for sexual assault.[8]

However, a church is not automatically liable for all criminal acts on its premises. For example, a child was raped in an Alabama church by a teenager living at the church. The church was not aware of any prior criminal behavior by the teenager. The child's mother sued the church for failure to supervise. The court dismissed the claim, based on the church's lack of knowledge of the risk.[9]

Volunteer Workers

A church can be liable for injuries to volunteers who are repairing the church building. For example, a volunteer painter at a Wisconsin church fell from a defective stepladder. He landed on the floor, fractured his skull, and sustained brain damage. His guardian successfully sued the church for providing an unsafe ladder.[10]

In South Carolina, a volunteer repairman slipped on an unsecured rafter in a church attic while attempting to fix the sound system. He fell ten feet through the ceiling to the concrete floor below. The jury awarded him $300,000 in damages. The church argued that the verdict should be overturned because the worker was a volunteer. The court disagreed. "Why should a church member be precluded from suing an association ... when a paid workman would be allowed to maintain an action for the very same injury?"[11]

However, like a visitor, a volunteer worker cannot recover if the danger was obvious. For example, a Missouri church member and volunteer fell from an unsecured ladder while repairing the church bell tower. He sued the church for his injuries. However, at trial, the church showed that the worker had helped set up the ladder and knew that it was unsecured. In fact, his knowledge of the danger was greater than the church's. Therefore, the church owed him no duty to warn of the danger, and the case was dismissed.[12]

Off-Premises Accidents

A church will seldom be liable for accidents occurring off of its property. For example, in Rhode Island, church parishioners were crossing the street following a church service to reach the lot where they had parked their car. They were struck by a drunk driver and seriously injured. The parishioners sued the church, claiming the church had failed to control traffic. The court dismissed the suit, applying the same legal principles as it would to any private landowner. The church had no liability for traffic control on the public street because that was "a duty allocated to the government, not to private individuals." The fact that the church could have asked the police to assign a traffic-control officer that evening did not create a duty for the church to do so.[13]

Improperly Correcting Hazard

Churches may be surprised to find that they have exposed themselves to additional liability by improperly *correcting* a hazard. For example, an Illinois pedestrian slipped and fell on a church's ice-covered steps and sued the church for her injuries. She showed that the ice was caused by the runoff of snow piled on adjoining stairs. The court held the church could be liable for the negligent removal of the snow. "While there is generally no duty to remove natural accumulations of ice and snow, a voluntary undertaking may subject defendant to liability if it is performed negligently."[14]

A church can even be sued for negligence in protecting against lightning! A Texas church purchased a lightning rod and cable system, but improperly installed two of the ground wires near a sidewalk. Lightning struck the rod, travelled down the cable, and a "side flash" struck a person on the sidewalk. The court held the church could be sued for the negligent installation of the lightning rod and cable.[15]

"Invitees" And "Licensees"
Some states require greater care be used to keep the church safe for invitees than for licensees. An "invitee" is a guest with a business purpose; a "licensee" is a guest without a business purpose. Interestingly, a church member is normally considered an "invitee," because of the member's regular financial support of the church. However, a visitor will normally be a "licensee."

This distinction arose when a person attending a family member's ordination service at a Florida church slipped on a heavily-waxed floor. The church had asked her to bring cookies to the service. The court held she was a licensee because the cookies were for the benefit of the minister and his family, not the church. As a result, the church could only be liable for her injuries if it had been guilty of "wilful and wanton" negligence.[16]

Similarly, an Alabama choir member slipped on a freshly-waxed floor while the choir was performing in another church's anniversary service. The court found she was a licensee because she did not provide a material financial benefit to the church she was visiting. "Such services benefit both the communities in which the churches are located and the visitors to the services, by providing spiritual direction and social fellowship." Thus, the visiting choir members were in much the same position as social guests "enjoying unrecompensed hospitality in a private home by invitation." Because the church had knowledge of the slippery condition, the visitor's claim against the church was dismissed.[17]

Charitable Immunity
Traditionally, charities were provided with broad immunity from lawsuits. Most states have now abandoned this rule. However, some states still provide limited immunity for churches and similar organizations.

For example, a New Jersey law bars negligence suits against charities by its "beneficiaries." A person attending a service in a New Jersey church slipped and fell in the parking lot. She brought suit against the church for her injuries. However, the court held the church attender was a "beneficiary" of the church, and therefore the claim was barred.[18]

Some states have immunity laws which cover informal non-profit recreational activities. For example, Wisconsin's Recreational Use Statute provides immunity for outdoor exercise and leisure activities. However, the immunity does not extend to a "sponsor" of an "organized team sports activity." A church paid a fee to reserve a local park for a Sunday afternoon picnic. A girl was injured in a softball game at the picnic, and her family sued the church. The family said the church should not be immune because it had "sponsored" the softball game. However, the court dismissed the suit, finding the game was a classic "pick-up" match rather than an "organized team sports activity."[19]

Similarly, Georgia's Recreational Property Act provides immunity for property owners who open the property to the public for free recreational use. A person was injured on a church swing and sued the church. The court held that the Act barred this claim, because the swing was open to the public and no fee was charged for its use.[20]

A church may lose its charitable immunity when conducting a for-profit activity. For example, an Ohio resident was injured while working at a church bazaar. The church argued it was entitled to charitable immunity because the bazaar did not make a large profit. The court rejected this defense, holding that there need not be a "substantial profit" before the church operation "ceases to be a charity."[21]

Vicarious Liability

As the previous cases have shown, your church will be liable for the conduct of its ministers, employees, and volunteers within the scope of their work for the church. The church cannot avoid liability by claiming that it was unaware of the individual's negligence. This is known by lawyers as "vicarious liability."

However, the courts have been more reluctant to extend liability up the "chain of command" to the denomination. For example, an Ohio church elder was in an auto accident which killed the other driver. The other driver's estate sued both the elder and the denomination. The court dismissed the claim against the denomination, because the elder was not the denomination's employee or subject to the denomination's day-to-day control.[22]

Similarly, a lawsuit against a Kansas diocese based on a parish pastor's auto accident was dismissed. The fact that the diocese had partial control over his employment and salary did not overcome the fact that the diocese lacked day-to-day control over the pastor's activities.[23]

Claims-Prevention Procedures

1. Snow should be promptly shoveled, especially before church events.
2. Wet floors should be immediately mopped.
3. If a hazard cannot be immediately corrected, place a prominent warning sign.
4. If neighborhood children play on the church property, erect a fence or place warning signs.
5. All safety devices at the church should be carefully tested.
6. Carefully supervise all church repair activities, including those done by volunteers.
7. If your state has some form of charitable immunity, ask your attorney what activities it covers.
8. Obtain a CGL insurance policy from your insurance agent. (See Chapter 6.)

Chapter 2
Clergy Malpractice

Most claims against your church for counseling negligence and "excessive discipline" will be barred by the First Amendment. However, not all clergy misconduct is immune from scrutiny.

The First Amendment embraces two concepts — freedom to believe and freedom to act. "The first is absolute but, in the nature of things, the second cannot be. Conduct remains subject to regulation for the protection of society."[24] Therefore, the courts may entertain claims against clergy for intentional misconduct.

Counseling Negligence

In the landmark case of *Nally v. Grace Community Church*, the California Supreme Court ruled that there could be no counseling-malpractice claim against a minister for failing to prevent a church member's suicide. First, the court noted that ministers do not claim to have the same training as psychologists and psychiatrists, and therefore cannot be judged by the same professional standard.

Second, the court held that establishing a separate standard for clergy would entangle the courts in evaluating religious doctrine. Imposing a duty of care on pastoral counseling "would necessarily be intertwined with the religious philosophy of the particular denomination or ecclesiastical teachings of the religious entity."[25]

Several states have followed the reasoning of *Nally* and refused to allow clergy-malpractice claims for counseling: Alabama, Arkansas, Colorado, Illinois, Nebraska, Ohio, Pennsylvania, and Utah.[26]

> *A priest or minister is not required to possess and apply the knowledge and use the skill and care ordinarily used by a reasonably well-qualified psychologist.*[27]

To date, no states have recognized such claims.[28]

Some states have not been willing to go as far as *Nally* in banning all counseling-malpractice claims against ministers. Instead, they have taken a more incremental approach, refusing to recognize malpractice under the facts before them.[29]

These states may be seeking to keep the door open for counseling malpractice if the minister has secular counseling credentials. For example, they might allow a malpractice claim against a minister who is also a licensed psychologist or psychiatrist. In such cases, though, the court would presumably refuse to evaluate the church doctrine, and instead would apply the secular professional standard. As one court noted:

> *[I]t is entirely possible that, in an age when many ecclesiastical organizations have assumed the task of providing a variety of medical and social services, a particular church might also offer purely secular counseling as a service to the members of its congregation or to a broader segment of the population ... If a church were to undertake such a project ... those who provided such professional services on behalf of the church would indeed be subject to the same legal strictures as those imposed upon individuals who undertake to provide such services in another setting.*[30]

This rule is no doubt correct. Therefore, a church's immunity to counseling-malpractice claims will not extend to church-sponsored psychological and psychiatric counseling services.

Church Discipline

Generally speaking, a church is insulated from liability for ecclesiastical disciplinary acts against its members. "Excessive discipline" claims against churches are normally dismissed because of the religious component involved in determining what is "excessive." For example, a parishioner sued for false imprisonment when a church told him his sins would not be forgiven if he did not remain in isolation for a week. The court dismissed the case, finding the church's teaching was protected religious speech.[31]

In part, courts defer to churches on matters of discipline because church membership is voluntary:

> *It is perfectly clear that, whatever church relationship is maintained in the United States, is not a matter of status ... It is based ... on voluntary consent ... A person who joins a church covenants expressly or impliedly that in consideration of the benefits which result from such a union he will submit to its control and be governed by its laws, usages and customs ...*[32]

For the same reason, church indoctrination and initiation procedures are not normally subject to judicial review. Thus, even the extreme "brainwashing" procedures used in the past by the Unification Church were generally immune from scrutiny.[33]

However, the implied consent to discipline generally ends when the member leaves the church. Thus, a member had no viable claim against an Oklahoma church for disciplinary action taken prior to her withdrawal. However, after she left the church, during a Sunday service, the elders read to the congregation some scriptures they believed she had violated. The court found this to be an actionable violation of her right of privacy, because she had withdrawn her consent to be subject to church discipline:

> *No real freedom to choose religion would exist in this land if under the shield of the First Amendment religious institutions could impose their will on the unwilling and claim immunity from secular judicature from their tortious acts.*[34]

"Wrongful Expulsion"

A church decision to expel a member will seldom be examined by a court, even if it affects the member's finances. For example, members of a Virginia church claimed that their church contributions were "expropriated" when they were expelled. The court rejected this argument, refusing to subject such ecclesiastical decisions to the scrutiny employed in secular matters.[35]

There is generally no claim against a church that "shuns" former members. For example, the Jehovah's Witnesses prohibit social contact with people who leave the church. A former Jehovah's Witness was shunned by several long-time friends who were church members. She brought suit against the church for the damage to her friendships caused by this practice. The court dismissed her claim, ruling that religious shunning cannot be prohibited by the courts. Assessing damages against the church for this practice "would in the long run have the same effect as prohibiting the practice and would compel the church to abandon part of its religious teachings." Thus, allowing such suits would violate the First Amendment by restricting the free exercise of religion.[36]

However, extreme cases of shunning may create legal liability, especially in a close-knit community. For example, a former Mennonite church member who was ostracized had a viable claim against the church for interference with marriage and business interests. The court allowed the claim because interference with the paramount state concern of protecting marriage and family outweighed the church's First Amendment rights.[37]

Defamation

There is generally no protection from defamation claims brought by non-church members. For example, a Maryland couple claimed that a minister falsely accused them of child abuse. In response to their defamation lawsuit, the minister asserted that his statements about their suspected child abuse were made in the course of his ministerial duties. The court refused to dismiss the lawsuit, finding the minister had the secular purpose of ruining the couple's reputation. The court noted, however, that there would have been immunity had the couple been church members and the minister's statements been part of church discipline. The consent to submit to church discipline is part of a "contract between the member and the church." There can be no legal claims for damage "incurred within the terms of the consent."[38]

In a report to the State of Alaska, a parishioner asserted that parish plans for an altar without a handrail constituted elder abuse or neglect. Her pastor then allegedly defamed her in a letter dismissing her from several volunteer positions. The court rejected the church's motion to dismiss. Evaluating whether the pastor's statements were true or false did not require the court to decide any religious questions.[39]

However, there can be no viable defamation claim for truthful statements. Thus, an excommunicated Iowa church member could not sue his former church for accurately informing the congregation that he had been excommunicated. Significantly, the congregation was not informed in detail of the grounds for his excommunication.[40]

Many states recognize a "qualified privilege" for non-malicious defamation occurring during the course of disciplinary proceedings.[41] For example, a Louisiana church board recommended their pastor be removed from the ministry, based on his unethical business dealings. He sued the board members for defamation. The court dismissed the lawsuit based on the qualified privilege for church disciplinary proceedings:

> *To allow defamation suits to be litigated to the fullest extent against members of a religious board who are merely discharging the duty which has been entrusted to them by their church could have a potentially chilling effect on the performance of those duties and could very well inhibit the free communication of important ideas and candid opinions.*[42]

For the same reason, inaccurate communications between two ministers about a person in their denomination will not constitute defamation unless they were motivated by malice. For example, one Baptist minister wrote to another to discuss the reasons a missionary was dismissed. The letter stated that the missionary was a liar who was attempting to destroy the denomination. As a result of this letter, the missionary was unable to obtain support from other Baptist churches. The missionary sued for libel. The court noted that the letter was written on a privileged occasion, and therefore held the missionary had to prove malice to prevail.[43]

Invasion Of Family Privacy

Courts have allowed churches to be sued for "invasion of privacy" in extreme cases of interference with family relations. For example, an Idaho husband and father brought a successful privacy suit against his former wife's church. The church had advised the wife that their marriage was not legitimate unless the husband belonged to the church. As a result, he alleged, the marriage broke up and the children were alienated from him. The church claimed such advice was protected under the First Amendment. However, the court found the church had engaged in bad-faith indoctrination practices with the intent to destroy the family, practices which were not protected from legal scrutiny. "Although free exercise of religion enjoys a high measure of constitutional protection and allows for proselytization, there are limits."[44]

Similarly, a Washington sect encouraged people to leave their spouses who were not members of the church. One person took this advice and divorced her husband. The husband sued the pastor and church for alienation of affections. The court rejected the church's First Amendment defense:

> *[O]ne does not, under the guise of exercising religious beliefs, acquire a license to wrongfully interfere with the familial relationships ... Ill will, intimidation, threats, or reckless recommendations of family separation directed toward alienating the spouses, where found to exist, nullify the privilege and project liability.*[45]

Emotional Distress

In extreme cases, the courts may allow emotional-distress claims based on excessive church discipline. For example, former disciples of the Unification Church claimed they were misled about the church's identity, then threatened with divine retribution if they left the church. The former disciples sued the church for intentional infliction of emotional distress. In response, the Unification

Church stated that the fraud was part of the free exercise of religion. The court rejected the church's defense:

> *[I]t is one thing when a person knowingly and voluntarily submits to a process involving coercive influence, as a novice does on entering a monastery or a seminary ... But it is quite another when a person is subject to coercive persuasion without his knowledge or consent.*[46]

Courts are more likely to allow emotional-distress claims if they do not require evaluation of church doctrine and discipline. A Utah church was sued for both clerical malpractice and intentional infliction of emotional distress. The court held there could be no claim for clergy malpractice, citing *Nally*. However, the court did allow the intentional infliction of emotional distress claim to proceed to trial.[47]

Normally, though, such claims are unsuccessful. A mother and daughter brought an emotional distress claim against the Hare Krishna Church for teaching the daughter that her family was an irrelevant and undesirable "entanglement in the material world." The mother and daughter asserted this teaching destroyed her family relationship. However, trial of their claim required evaluating the Krishna movement's religious beliefs and writings. Therefore, the court held that the claim was barred by the First Amendment. "The [Krishna movement] cannot be forced to choose between censoring its religious scriptures to remove material which may be offensive to contemporary society and paying tort damages for the privilege of maintaining unpopular religious beliefs."[48]

Claims-Prevention Procedures

1. If the church offers psychological or psychiatric services, you should obtain an appropriate malpractice insurance policy. (See Chapter 6.)

2. Provide a written notice to people who receive regular counseling, clarifying that the church is not providing psychological or psychiatric services.

3. The church should keep information disclosed in counseling sessions strictly confidential.

4. Volunteer church counselors should be fully trained and "backed up" by a referral network of pastoral and professional counselors.
5. Do not charge for counseling services.
6. Church discipline should be done in full consultation with church leadership and with careful documentation.
7. Use discretion when discussing negative information about former church members.

Chapter 3

Sex Abuse

A church's immunity for counseling malpractice may not extend to sexual misconduct in connection with counseling, or to sexual abuse of minors. Many courts consider this to be a secular matter independent of church doctrine. Liability for sex abuse may also extend beyond the individual abuser to superiors who know or should know of the abuse.

Breach Of Fiduciary Duty

A "fiduciary duty" is a duty of loyalty and good faith owed in a confidential or professional relationship. Some states allow sex abuse victims to sue clergy for breach of fiduciary duty, while others do not. Those that allow the claims reason that "neutral principles" can be applied:

> *[I]nasmuch as it is conduct, and not creed, that underlies plaintiffs' actions, and that the potential for civil consequences exists equally as to religious and non-religious persons, and as to clergy and lay persons of all religions alike, the Free Exercise aspect of the First Amendment does not come into play to preclude plaintiffs' [breach of fiduciary duty action].*[49]

For example, a parishioner claimed the pastor had seduced her during a counseling relationship. She sued the pastor and church for intentional infliction of emotional distress. The church asked the court to dismiss the lawsuit on First Amendment grounds, arguing that it was essentially a claim for clerical malpractice. The court agreed that claims for clerical malpractice were impermissible. However, it found that the parishioner potentially had a secular claim for breach of fiduciary duty — for violating a "special relationship of trust and confidence."[50] The court did not explain how the scope and nature of this relationship could be determined without examining church doctrine and practice.

States that prohibit breach of fiduciary duty claims reason that defining the degree of trust appropriate to a religious "fiduciary" would entangle the courts in religious doctrine:

> *[This] would require the court and the jury to consider the fundamental perspective and approach to counseling inherent in the beliefs and practices of that denomination. This is as unconstitutional as it is impossible.*[51]

For example, a church member claimed her pastor engaged in improper sexual contact during counseling sessions. She sued the pastor and the church for breach of fiduciary duty. The court dismissed the claim, holding it was "simply an elliptical way of alleging clergy malpractice." It would be impossible to define in secular terms the scope of a fiduciary duty between church member and clergy, because that relationship is "clearly rooted in the tenets and internal organization of [the] religion."[52]

Negligent Hiring And Supervision

Some states will not extend liability for sex abuse beyond the individual abuser. For example, a Wisconsin parishioner had been sexually abused by a priest. She brought suit against the archdiocese for negligently hiring, supervising, and retaining the priest. The Wisconsin Supreme Court rejected the claim, holding that determining the archdiocese's responsibility would require evaluating church doctrine on the qualification of priests and the standards for repentance, inquiries which are forbidden by the First Amendment.[53]

However, most states will hold churches liable for negligent hiring or supervision, if the supervisors knew the individual was potentially dangerous.[54] For example, a parishioner who was sexually abused by a Colorado priest sued the diocese and bishop for negligent hiring. The court rejected the defense that such a claim violated the First Amendment, finding that neutral principles can be used to evaluate negligent-hiring claims against churches. The court then held that employers such as the diocese may have a heightened duty of care when hiring someone for a position of trust:

> *The requisite degree of care increases, and may require expanded inquiry into the employee's background, when the employer expects the employee to have frequent contact with the public or when the nature of the employment fosters close contact and a special relationship between particular persons and the employee.*[55]

The jury found that the diocese had breached this duty to adequately inquire into the priest's background and awarded the abuse victim $1,216,500 in damages against the diocese and bishop.

An Ohio woman claimed she had been raped by a pastor during a counseling session. She sued the church for negligent hiring. The court agreed with her contention that a church could be liable for carelessly hiring an employee:

> *[E]ven the most liberal construction of the First Amendment will not protect a religious organization's decision to hire someone who it knows is likely to commit criminal or tortious acts.*

However, the court dismissed the suit, finding no evidence the pastor had a history of sexual misconduct or criminal activity.[56]

Similarly, a Michigan priest was sexually abusing seminary students. The court held the priest's superiors would be liable for negligent hiring and supervision if they had known of the problem. However, the students presented no evidence that the school or religious supervisors had been notified of the abuse. Therefore, the claims against the school and supervisors were dismissed.[57]

Other Theories Against Supervisors

Under the doctrine of "vicarious liability," a church or church organization will be liable for harm caused by pastors or other church employees within the scope of their employment. However, a church organization will not be liable for unforeseeable sexual abuse. A woman who alleged she was sexually abused by Catholic priests sued the Archbishop of Los Angeles. The court dismissed the claim against the archbishop, finding no evidence that he could have foreseen the alleged abuse. "It would defy every notion of logic and fairness to say that sexual activity between a priest and a parishioner is characteristic ... of the Catholic church."[58]

An Arkansas woman obtained a verdict of $1.5 million against a priest who sexually abused her as a child. She then sought payment from the priest's religious society, arguing that the society had an implied (unwritten) contract to pay his debts. However, the only evidence she produced at trial was that the society agreed to pay its priests' necessary living expenses. The court found this was not the same as a promise to "pay every debt of its priests no matter what the circumstances." Therefore, she was denied recovery against the society.[59]

In theory, a church can be liable for sex abuse by a volunteer worker who was acting as the church's "servant." The principal feature of a servant is the church's right to control the volunteer's activities. For example, a 14-year-old girl was molested by a church volunteer, and her family obtained a $170,000 judgment against the volunteer. The family sought to hold the church jointly liable. However, the court rejected the claim against the church, finding no evidence that the volunteer was subject to the church's instructions or that the molestation had occurred during the scope of the volunteer's church-ordered duties.[60]

Statute Of Limitations And Delayed Discovery

In many states, the statute of limitations for sexual abuse does not begin to run until the victim knows or should know of the abuse. This "delayed discovery" rule prevents the statute of limitations from expiring in cases of repressed memory.

The "delayed discovery" rule is seldom applied to adults, even those with psychological problems. For example, a woman with multiple personality disorder brought a sex abuse claim against an

Oklahoma priest twenty years after the abuse. The statute of limitations for those claims was two years. The court dismissed her claim, holding that her disorder was discoverable and thus did not excuse her delay in bringing suit.[61]

Claims-Prevention Procedures

1. To reduce false accusations of sex abuse, one-on-one counseling should be avoided or conducted at the church during business hours.

2. The church must promptly investigate any claim or rumor of sex abuse by church pastors, employees, or volunteers. Your attorney should be promptly informed and the accused worker should be suspended until the claim is resolved.

3. Interviews and background checks should be performed for all prospective church employees.

4. Have your attorney prepare a criminal record check form for all employees and volunteers to sign.

5. If sex abuse is confirmed, the worker should be immediately terminated.

6. The church bylaws should provide for the expulsion of members who engage in sex abuse, and those bylaws should be strictly enforced.

Chapter 4
Employment Disputes

Generally speaking, your church cannot avoid neutral or secular employment laws of general applicability.[62] However, employment laws will not be enforced if they would create excessive entanglement with religion. Thus, claims against your church involving core questions of church discipline and internal governance are outside the scope of judicial review.[63]

Hierarchical/Congregational

The degree to which a court may become involved in a church employment dispute is affected by whether the church is "hierarchical" or "congregational." A hierarchial church is a subordinate member of a denomination with "superior ecclesiastical tribunals" which have "a general and ultimate power of control more or less complete" over the individual churches.[64] A congregational church is one "strictly independent of other ecclesiastical organizations."[65]

In a hierarchical church, civil courts generally lack authority to hear employment disputes. Instead, they defer to the denomination.[66] In a congregational church, the courts have a "secular" issue they may address — whether the employment decision was made by the proper church authority.[67]

Where there is a dispute as to whether the church is hierarchical or congregational in nature, the trial court will first resolve that question. This initial inquiry is not prohibited by the First Amendment. To make this determination, the court is permitted to evaluate religious documents.[68]

Hiring Of Clergy

Courts will almost never inquire into a church's reasons for rejecting an individual for pastorship. Thus, a Maryland minister claimed she had suffered from hiring discrimination. The court refused to hear the case, stating that the First Amendment prohibited such an inquiry:

> *We cannot imagine an area of inquiry less suited to a temporal court for decision; evaluation of the "gifts and graces" of a minister must be left to ecclesiastical institutions.*[69]

A Colorado ministerial intern was denied a pastorate after she filed a sexual harassment claim. She sued the church under the Federal Civil Rights Act, which prohibits employers from retaliating against employees who file harassment complaints. The court dismissed the case, ruling that such an inquiry would inevitably require entanglement in religious doctrine. Even if church doctrine was merely a "pretext" to cover sexual harassment, the court did not want to evaluate the sincerity of the pretext.[70]

Discharge Of Clergy

Most states will not consider a pastor's wrongful discharge claim against a church, even if the church violated its own procedures and laws. For example, a Michigan pastor was discharged by his denomination over his alleged misconduct as trustee of an estate. He brought suit for reinstatement and damages, claiming the denomination had not followed its own procedures. However, the court dismissed his case, deferring to the final decision of the denomination.[71]

Likewise, a priest's claim for wrongful discharge against a religious hospital was barred. The priest had been employed as a chaplain at a church-affiliated hospital. She was fired for violating certain canonical laws, and brought suit for age and sex discrimination. The court dismissed the suit. "Personnel decisions by church-affiliated institutions affecting clergy are *per se* religious matters and cannot be reviewed by civil courts."[72]

Similarly, the courts refused to become involved in a Texas minister's claim that the denomination improperly terminated his license. The minister asserted that the court could use neutral principles to determine whether the denomination had violated its own rules. However, the court held that the substance of the claim was church discipline and government, into which the courts cannot intrude. "[T]he interaction between a church and its pastor is an integral part of church government."[73]

The same rationale is used with ministerial interns. For example, an intern claimed an Iowa church violated its established procedure by discharging him without an opportunity to correct deficiencies in his ministry. The court dismissed his lawsuit based on the First Amendment prohibition of judicial interference with "ecclesiastical decision making."[74]

In rare cases, when the issues are purely secular, a court will agree to hear a pastor's wrongful-termination claim. For example, an Idaho pastor who was fired by his church sought damages for breach of the employment contract. The church argued that the reasons for his discharge were primarily ecclesiastical. The court refused to examine the merits of any ecclesiastical considerations, but allowed trial on the question of whether the church had in fact acted for ecclesiastical reasons. The jury found that the pastor had been wrongly terminated, and awarded him roughly four months of salary and insurance premiums as damages.[75]

Non-Clergy

Courts have been more willing to entertain employment discrimination claims by non-clergy employees of religious organizations. Enforcement of a religious organization's employment contracts does not violate the First Amendment where the person did not perform ministerial functions and compliance with religious doctrine was not a condition of the contract.

For example, nuns who taught at a Catholic university claimed they were fired without receiving the "terminal year" contracts promised in their employment agreements. The school stated the First Amendment precluded judicial scrutiny because the nuns were performing ministerial functions. The court rejected the school's defense, noting there were no provisions in their employment contracts which imposed religious obligations on the school's teachers. As a result, the nuns were each awarded $45,000 as compensation for their lost wages.[76]

Outside of the church-pastor relationship, the court's decision whether to abstain will depend largely on the intent of the parties in the employment contract. The courts will examine three factors to determine whether the parties intended control of the employment decision to depend on doctrinal matters.

First, such an intent may be clear from the language of a written employment contract. For example, an employment agreement may authorize discharge for public repudiation of church doctrine.[77]

Second, the intent may be shown by the creation of a religious tribunal for adjudication of such disputes.[78] As noted earlier in the chapter, these tribunals are frequently created at the denominational level.

Third, the intent may be shown by the nature of the employee's duties:

> As a general rule, if the employee's primary duties consist of teaching, spreading the faith, church governance, supervision of a religious order, or supervision or participation in religious ritual and worship, he or she should be considered "clergy."[79]

The fact that someone is an ordained minister does not preclude litigation if he or she was not employed in a pastoral position. The "ministerial exception to [discrimination laws] does not depend upon ordination but upon the function of the position."[80]

EEOC

An employee may enlist the help of the Equal Employment Opportunity Commission (EEOC) to bring suit against employers that violate discrimination laws. On occasion, the EEOC will sue a religious organization for discrimination. When deciding whether to hear such suits, the courts will use the same basic criteria as for a private discrimination claim.

For example, EEOC claims will seldom be allowed against clergy. In particular, seminary professors hired largely on religious criteria and teaching no purely secular courses will normally be treated as clergy. For example, higher education institutions are required to file detailed information reports with the EEOC concerning their employees' race, gender, salaries, and tenure status. A seminary refused to file this form on First Amendment grounds. The EEOC sued the seminary to require compliance with the reporting requirement. The court held that the seminary professors were "ministers," and therefore were not subject to the reporting requirement. However, the seminary was required to file the report for its support staff and other non-ministers.[81]

A religious organization cannot offer different benefits to non-clergy male and female employees unless it can show a compelling religious interest. A California religious school provided health insurance only to "heads of households." In practice this meant single people and married men, because of the organization's belief that a husband was financially responsible for his family. A married female employee of the school filed a sex-discrimination claim with the EEOC and prevailed. The court rejected the school's argument that the insurance preference was based on its religious belief about family responsibility, finding the "minimal" interference with religious exercise to be outweighed by the "compelling" government interest in eliminating discrimination.[82]

A religious organization's prohibition of lawsuits by members of an affiliated church may also run afoul of discrimination laws and the EEOC. For example, a publishing company affiliated with the Seventh-Day Adventist Church required its employees to be church members. The company paid lower benefit levels to its female employees than its male employees. An editorial secretary at the company filed suit with the EEOC for sex discrimination for the difference in benefits. The company then fired the secretary for violating church doctrine prohibiting members from suing the church. The EEOC brought suit against the publishing company for retaliatory discharge. The court agreed with the EEOC, rejecting the company's argument that it should be permitted to establish church doctrine prohibiting litigation:

> *To permit the various Adventist institutions to retaliate against employees who challenge discrimination through EEOC procedures would defeat Congress' intention to protect employees of religious employers.*[83]

Interestingly, the court did not address the public interest in enforcing agreements to avoid litigation. (See Chapter 7)

Labor Relations In Church Schools

The National Labor Relations Board (NLRB) governs union bargaining activities at public and private schools. However, in 1979, the United States Supreme Court ruled that NLRB supervision of parochial schools normally violates the First Amendment:

> *The church-teacher relationship in a church-operated school differs from the employment relationship in a public or other non-religious school. We see no escape from conflicts flowing from the [NLRB's] exercise of jurisdiction over teachers in church-operated schools and the consequent serious First Amendment questions that would follow.*[84]

Thus, collective-bargaining laws will not be enforced when the interference with religious education is direct. For example, a suit to require collective bargaining in Illinois and Indiana Catholic schools was rejected as interfering with the bishops' control over the religious curriculum. To minimize friction with the government, the court noted, the bishops would tailor their conduct and decisions to "steer far wider of the unlawful zone" of interfering with the rights of union members.[85]

However, collective-bargaining laws may be enforceable against religious organizations if the interference with religion is "incidental."[86] For example, a New York teachers' union filed charges with the state's labor relations board alleging that parochial school managers engaged in unfair labor practices. The board claimed that such an action would have a chilling effect on the school's exercise of religion. However, the court found this indirect burden on religion outweighed by the "compelling state interest" in ensuring collective bargaining.

Other Claims

A church may be subject to suit for disclosing confidential information about its employees. An associate pastor in a Maryland church went through a church employee's files, found letters indicating that she was having an affair, and told various members of the church. The employee sued the church for damages. The court allowed the lawsuit to proceed, finding the associate pastor had unreasonably intruded upon the employee's private concerns.[87]

A classic example of judicial restraint is the assignment of pastors or priests to a particular congregation. For example, a Michigan priest encountered resistance from his largely Polish congregation when he removed Polish religious artifacts from the church and made other reforms. He then refused communion to one of his critics. Parishioners brought suit against the bishop, seeking removal of the priest and damages for emotional distress. The court refused to hear the case. "Whenever the court must stray into questions of religious doctrine or ecclesiastical policy, the court loses jurisdiction."[88]

A parochial school teacher can bring an age discrimination action against the school. An older math teacher at a Catholic high school was fired, and he brought suit under the Age Discrimination in Employment Act. The school claimed he was dismissed for reasons unrelated to his age, including failure to begin classes with prayer and failure to attend Mass with his students. The school argued that to distinguish between the religious and secular reasons for the teacher's discharge would entangle the government in religion. The court rejected this argument, finding that the narrow scope of inquiry would not interfere with the school's religious activities.[89]

Claims-Prevention Procedures

1. Do not let threats or concerns about discrimination lawsuits intimidate your church when selecting senior and associate pastors. Choose the best-qualified people.

2. Have your attorney review all church employment letters and contracts to ensure there are no unintended limitations on the church's ability to fire the employee.

3. Provide all church employees with written annual performance reviews.

4. Have each church employee sign an agreement that they will report within thirty days any discriminatory or illegal conduct.

5. Include in all employment contracts the express provision that the church may fire the employee for adultery, dishonesty, or public repudiation of church doctrine.

Chapter 5

Property Disputes

You should expect court involvement in legal disputes concerning the ownership of church property. Property disputes are the kind of church-related cases courts may consider. As one court explained:

> *Churches are viewed in two parts. The first is the spiritual including the doctrine and the basic beliefs of the church. The second is the temporal including its real property and the income used for its general operations. The courts ... with great reluctance, will resolve issues relating to the latter but not the former.*[90]

In practice, the courts are seldom "reluctant" to decide property disputes. Instead, as with employment disputes, the courts employ two rules to resolve these cases: (1) deference to the denomination, and (2) neutral principles.

Deference Rule

When a religious controversy is a component of a property dispute, the court will normally defer to the decision of the highest church body on that issue. As the United States Supreme Court stated in 1969:

> *First Amendment values are plainly jeopardized when church property litigation is made to turn on the resolution by civil courts of controversies over religious doctrine and practice.*[91]

For example, the church district ordered an Illinois church closed because of declining membership. The district conveyed the church's real estate to one family. The church bylaws did not allow the district to liquidate the property until the church ceased to function as a church. The church's former trustees objected to this conveyance, asserting that they had not ceased to function as a church. However, the court deferred to the district on this issue, because it was "the highest church body to decide the issue."[92]

Members of a denomination have implicitly contracted to be bound by the denominational authority.[93] The rationale for this contractual approach is to enable people to affiliate themselves for religious purposes without court interference.[94]

However, deference to church hierarchy has its limits. Courts recognize the danger of absolute deference to denominations in secular matters:

> The deference approach assumes that the local church has relinquished control to the hierarchial body in all cases ... Such a practice ... discourages local churches from associating with a hierarchial church for purposes of religious worship out of fear of losing their property ...[95]

Neutral Principles

When religious matters are not at issue, courts may decide property disputes between church organizations. However, the U.S. Supreme Court has ruled, the courts must rely "exclusively on objective, well-established concepts of trust and property law familiar to lawyers and judges."[96] The Supreme Court noted:

> The State has an obvious and legitimate interest in the peaceful resolution of property disputes, and in providing a civil forum where the ownership of church property can be determined conclusively.[97]

Thus, the courts will not defer to an ecclesiastical determination of property ownership where no "doctrinal controversy is involved."[98]

In practice, courts seldom abstain from deciding church property disputes, because of the practical need to clarify title for future purchasers:

Were it otherwise, controversies . . . might never be resolved, and the title to the church property would be enmeshed in a quagmire from which extrication would be nearly impossible. Title to property cannot be allowed to drift about in an atmosphere of uncertainty.[99]

Under this "neutral principles" analysis, the courts may examine the local church's charter and bylaws. When a denomination is involved, the court may also examine the denomination's charter and constitution. However, for property held by a local church, the courts will generally give priority to the local church's charter and bylaws if they give the local church the exclusive right to dispose of its property.[100]

Withdrawal From Denomination

Questions over property ownership frequently arise when a church withdraws from its denomination or parent church. When this occurs, the "neutral principles of law" standard calls "for the completely secular examination of deeds to the church property, state statutes and existing local and general church constitutions, by-laws, canons, Books of Discipline and the like to determine whether any basis for a trust in favor of the general church exists."[101]

Often, a local church's articles of incorporation provide that it holds property in trust for the denomination or that property will "revert" to the denomination. These provisions will normally require a church to relinquish property rights upon withdrawal from the denomination.

For example, a Maryland church withdrew from a parent church and claimed ownership over two parcels of land that had been sold to the local church. The deeds conveying the property to the local church made no mention of ownership reverting to the parent church. However, the local church's 1894 articles of incorporation provided that it held property in "trust" for the parent church. Consequently, the court ruled that the two parcels reverted to the parent church when the local church withdrew.[102]

Many states recognize an implied trust, under certain circumstances, between a parent and local church. For example, a Connecticut congregation which left the Episcopal Church sought to retain ownership over the church property. The congregation noted that there was no provision in any church documents stating that its property was held in trust for the Episcopal Church. The congregation also noted that they were responsible to manage and control the property. However, the court found that an implied trust existed, based on the centralized hierarchy of the Episcopal Church and the practice of the Episcopal Church that property could not be sold without the Bishop's consent. As a result, the departing congregation forfeited its property to the denomination.[103]

However, a requirement that the denomination consent to the sale of property, by itself, will not create an implied trust relationship. For example, after a South Dakota church withdrew from a national denomination, the denomination sought control over the local church's property. The denomination's constitution limited the local church's use of its property while it was a member of the denomination, but did not discuss disposition of the property in case of withdrawal. Nothing in the local church's charter gave the denomination control over the property. Therefore, the court ruled that there was no implied trust, and that the local church owned the property after withdrawal.[104]

Some states do not recognize implied trusts. They require an express trust provision before finding the departing church has forfeited property to the denomination. For example, the California courts have concluded that an implied trust theory violates the First Amendment, requiring courts to evaluate the inherently religious issue of the relationship between local and parent churches. "[T]he difficulties ... in use of the implied trust theory, once evaluation of theology and doctrine has been forbidden, remain insurmountable."[105]

Congregational Splits

The same property-ownership principles apply when a church congregation has split. In a congregational church, ownership is determined by the church's articles and bylaws.

However, in a hierarchical church, ownership normally remains with the members who remain in the denomination. "[T]hose members who renounce their allegiance to the church lose any rights in the property involved and the property belongs to the members who remain loyal to the church."[106]

In a hierarchical church, the denomination rather than the courts may have jurisdiction to resolve disputes between a church's conflicting factions. However, control by the denomination is not automatic, and the articles and bylaws of the local church and denomination may be dispositive.

Unfortunately, in many cases, those documents are silent or ambiguous on the subject. For example, in Illinois a regional diocese dismissed a local church's directors and appointed other members to a commission to govern the church. The diocese then ordered the former directors to deliver the church's assets and records to the newly appointed commission members. The former directors refused, and the new commission members took them to court. The court was unable to determine from the church documents whether the diocese had jurisdiction in the matter. Neither the local church's articles of incorporation nor the diocese's bylaws defined the diocese's jurisdiction over property disputes. Therefore, a trial was required to determine the diocese's jurisdiction, including testimony of any verbal agreements between the diocese and local church to clarify the ambiguity.[107]

Financial Information

A suit for an accounting of church funds is a property dispute which can normally be resolved by application of neutral legal principles. Thus, it was proper for the California Attorney General to intervene in the administration of a charitable trust even though the trustee was a religious organization.[108]

Members of an Arkansas church went to court to obtain disclosure of financial data and other business information about the church. The court dismissed the case, holding that resolution of the dispute would involve critiquing the church teaching that its elders had sole responsibility for church finances. "Internal church disputes relating to the disclosure of church business should not be subject to the legal concerns of this court."[109]

However, church business records are not automatically immune from scrutiny. If there is no relevant church doctrine, the courts may require their disclosure. Members of a Louisiana church were successful in obtaining a court-ordered disclosure of financial information. There was no church doctrine precluding the members from obtaining the information. Therefore, the court enforced the state's law requiring all nonprofit corporations to disclose basic financial information.[110]

Judicial Officers

Some courts will examine the regularity of church procedure when property rights are subject to deprivation. For example, a faction in a Virginia congregational church claimed they were not allowed to speak in opposition to the church's building a senior citizens home and that the pastor improperly counted "absentee cards" that favored the project. The faction petitioned the court to have a special commissioner appointed to oversee the vote. The court agreed to appoint the commissioner, finding that the dissenters' property rights were at risk.[111]

Other states which have authorized judicial officers to oversee difficult congregational meetings include California, Kentucky, New York, and Texas.[112]

These cases seem inconsistent with the principle that donations to a church are gifts that sever the donor's property rights:

> *[T]he donor has no right to retrieve, control or direct the manner in which the money ... given shall be used simply because he has made such contributions to the church, nor because he is a member of the class which may be benefited by the carrying out of its purposes.*[113]

Copyrights And Trademarks

Churches are not exempt from the copyright and trademark laws that apply to other people and organizations. These laws simply protect the ownership rights of the ideas — they are not concerned with the accuracy of the ideas. Thus, to enforce a church's copyright does not foster the "establishment" of that organization's religion and does not interfere with the free exercise of religion.

For example, an Arizona religious organization sued an author for copyright infringement, because the author was copying and distributing its religious text without authorization or compensation. The author claimed enforcement of the copyright laws would violate the First Amendment by interfering with her practice of religion. The court rejected this argument, finding the copyright laws to be "neutral laws of general applicability to which the defendant must adhere for the betterment of the public good."[114]

Similarly, a religious instructor directed her students to copy a religious organization's books and audio tapes after the organization refused to sell her the books and tapes. The instructor asserted that the copying prohibition restricted her free exercise of religion. The court rejected this defense, and found her in violation of the copyright laws.[115]

Claims-Prevention Procedures

1. Obtain legal advice about church property before joining or leaving a denomination.

2. If your church belongs to a denomination, review your church's articles and bylaws to be sure they accurately state your intentions about denominational ownership over church property.

3. Review your church's articles and bylaws to be sure they spell out procedures for resolving property issues if the church splits.

4. Be sure your church's articles or bylaws state the circumstances under which members may review church financial information.

5. Have your attorney review with you the limitations on church copying of copyrighted documents.

Chapter 6

Liability Insurance Policies

"Liability" insurance is the coverage that protects you from a lawsuit. If the lawsuit falls within the policy's coverages, it both pays the lawyer to defend you and pays for the judgment or settlement. For churches, the principal liability insurance policies to consider are CGL, D and O, employment practices, malpractice, automobile, and umbrella.

CGL

The Commercial General Liability (CGL) policy is the standard business liability policy. For churches, its principal coverages are for non-employees injured on church property, for defamation, and for negligent supervision of church workers.

The CGL policy contains four basic liability coverages: bodily injury, property damage, personal injury, and advertising injury. Most CGL claims are for the first two coverages — bodily injury and property damage.

The bodily injury and property damage coverages do not include claims of intentional misconduct. However, they will usually cover the church against negligent supervision of its employees and volunteers who engaged in intentional misconduct such as sex abuse.[116]

CGL policies will seldom cover punitive damages. For example, a Minnesota diocese was sued for the negligent and reckless supervision of one of its priests, who sexually abused several children. The victims were awarded $812,250 in traditional compensatory damages, plus $200,000 in punitive damages. There was coverage for the negligent and reckless supervision claims.

However, the court refused to extend coverage for the punitive damages. "As a general rule, insurance coverage for punitive damages is void as against public policy."[117]

The "personal injury" and "advertising injury" coverages are narrowly construed. Thus, a false advertising claim against a church will seldom be covered unless it constitutes "unfair competition" with a competitor. For example, a church foundation built a residential development for senior citizens, financed by city bonds. When the project failed, several investors sued the church for negligently misrepresenting the project's viability. The church sought coverage under the "advertising liability" portion of its CGL policy, characterizing the lawsuit as one for "unfair competition." The court rejected the church's coverage claim because there was no "injury inflicted on a competitor."[118] The standard CGL policy after 1986 has eliminated coverage for unfair competition.

"Personal injury" coverage includes claims of libel and slander. (Collectively these are known as "defamation.") This is important insurance for a church. However, the defamation coverage is narrowly construed. Therefore, a defamation claim may not be paid if it was incidental to another, uncovered claim.[119]

Some CGL insurers will allow the church's officers and directors to be named as co-insureds on the church's policy, or will define "insured" to automatically include officers and directors. However, this provides little additional coverage. If the claim against the church would not be covered, then the claim against an officer or director would not be covered.[120]

Additionally, if individuals are named as co-insureds, coverage for the individuals will normally be strictly limited to their duties within the religious organization. For example, a CGL policy for the St. Louis Archdiocese and its priests only covered the priests while "acting within the scope of their respective duties." This was held to exclude injuries to a police officer while a priest was picketing at an abortion clinic.

> *The fact that [he] was a priest 24 hours a day does not make the Archdiocese responsible for all his activities, and does not make any and all of his activities the actions of a priest within the scope of his respective duties.*[121]

Similarly, the CGL policy will seldom cover individual church employees who engage in misconduct away from the church or outside the scope of church duties. For example, a Louisiana priest sought coverage under his church's CGL policy for a claim that he sexually abused a minor in Mississippi. The court found no coverage, finding the priest was "well outside [the] parameters" of his duties for the church.[122]

D And O

A directors and officers ("D and O") policy protects the church's officers and directors from lawsuits naming the officers or directors as defendants.

Although a D and O policy will not cover lawsuits against the church, it will reimburse the church for any obligation it has to indemnify (pay judgments against) its officers or directors. A church may have a duty to indemnify which is express (contained in the bylaws or other church documents) or implied (based on the church's words and conduct and the nature of the person's relationship with the church).

D and O policies generally do not provide a defense for the officers and directors. Instead, they will reimburse the attorneys' fees. Thus, the church and its officers and directors must finance their own defense, keep copies of the attorney billings, and submit the bills to the insurer.

Most D and O policies exclude claims for bodily injury and emotional distress. This precludes coverage for a large percentage of the claims against churches.

Most D and O policies also contain an "insured vs. insured" exclusion. This means there is no coverage for lawsuits between the officers and directors who are insured under the policy.

While most D and O policies have the same basic coverages, there is no standard policy. Therefore, you will want to carefully discuss the options with your insurance agent.

Employment Practices

The Employment Practices Liability policy is a new policy offered by several insurers to fill in certain gaps in the CGL policy.

In particular, the Employment Practices policy expressly covers discrimination and wrongful discharge.

Unfortunately, most insurers' versions of the Employment Practices policy exclude intentional acts. Most discrimination and wrongful discharge is intentional. Thus, it is unclear whether the Employment Practices policy will provide much coverage beyond the standard CGL policy.

Malpractice

"Malpractice" policies cover claims for the negligent performance of professional services. As previously noted, clergy are generally not liable for malpractice. However, if your church offers professional services such as psychological or psychiatric counseling, you will want to obtain a suitable malpractice policy from your insurance agent.

Malpractice policies generally exclude claims for conduct which is fraudulent, malicious, criminal, or defamatory. For clergy, these are the principal kinds of malpractice claims which are permitted. Therefore, a malpractice policy will provide little meaningful protection to the average church.

Auto

Like a business, a church needs automobile insurance for its employees and vehicles. Check with your insurance agent to be sure volunteers are covered while driving church vehicles.

Automobile policies will provide liability insurance for bodily injury and property damage claims. Most states require minimum liability limits such as $25,000, but you can purchase higher limits than the minimum.

Most policies also include coverage for accidents with uninsured and underinsured motorists. However, these coverages are only triggered if the other driver was at fault. For example, a church van was involved in an automobile accident in North Carolina. A passenger of the van was injured, and the other vehicle's insurer paid her the policy limits. She then sued the church's insurance company for underinsured benefits, to collect the difference. However, her complaint stated that the driver of the church van was the sole cause of the accident. The court denied her coverage claim. "Since plaintiff contends that the van driver was the 'sole' cause of the accident, obviously ... the other driver ... had nothing to do with it. Without liability on [the other driver's] part, there can be no claim for under-insured motorist coverage."[123]

Specialty Policies

Particular insurers may offer unusual or specialized policies that do not fit into the above categories. Often these can provide useful coverages.

For example, a Massachusetts theological school was insured under a board of education liability policy. A tenured professor successfully sued the school, proving that he had been recklessly fired in violation of the Age Discrimination In Employment Act. The insurer denied coverage, even though the policy contained no exclusion for reckless or intentional acts. Like most states, Massachusetts does not allow coverage for intentional acts. However, because the claim was for reckless rather than intentional conduct, the court found coverage for the lawsuit. The insurer was required to pay approximately $500,000 for the judgment and over $100,000 the school had incurred in attorneys' fees to defend the claim.[124]

Umbrella

Excess or "umbrella" policies are frequently purchased to extend the limits of a church's existing liability policies. For example, a church's auto policy may have liability limits of $100,000. Its umbrella policy can then provide coverage from $100,000 to $25 million.[125]

Because large claims are relatively rare, insurers can provide umbrella policies for little additional premium.

Conclusion

As set forth above, the essential liability policies for a church are CGL and auto, perhaps with an umbrella policy to increase the limits. For many churches, there will be little benefit to purchasing a standard D and O, malpractice, or employment practices liability policy.

However, your insurance agent may be able to get a policy from a particular insurer with broader coverages. If you are willing to pay enough premiums, you can obtain insurance for almost any risk. Thus, use this chapter as a starting place to know what questions to ask your agent.

Chapter 7

Arbitration And Mediation

Most courts strongly encourage the alternate dispute resolution (ADR) methods of arbitration and mediation to reduce court congestion. ADR must be agreed to by all parties, either before or after the dispute developed.

Arbitration involves the submission of a dispute to a third person — the arbitrator — for a final determination of the conflict. In mediation, by contrast, the third person (the mediator) does not determine the outcome. Instead, the mediator facilitates negotiations between the parties.

ADR is especially appropriate in church-based disputes. As noted in previous chapters, the American courts frequently defer to a denomination's internal dispute resolution processes on both religious and secular issues.[126]

Courts may actively encourage parties to religious disputes to use ADR. An English-speaking church started a mission to its city's Hispanic community, resulting in the creation of a Hispanic congregation which used the parent church's facilities. A dispute arose over whether the Hispanic congregation were members of the parent church, because they had not followed the procedures in the church bylaws of a vote by the deacons and the congregation. Two attempts were made to resolve the dispute by ADR. First, the Hispanic members requested binding arbitration by the denomination, but the parent church rejected the denomination's authority in the matter. Second, the court suggested that the Hispanic members apply for membership through the traditional channels, but they did not agree to that procedure. The court then agreed to decide the membership issue through a conventional lawsuit.[127]

This chapter will examine the history of arbitration and mediation, then discuss the ADR services of the Institute for Christian Conciliation and the American Arbitration Association.

Arbitration

Arbitration has been described as "the oldest known method of settlement of disputes between men."[128] One authority has traced back the practice of arbitration to King Solomon in 1 Kings 3:16-28, when he resolved the dispute between two women over a baby:

> *King Solomon was an arbitrator, and it is interesting to note that the procedure used by him was in many respects similar to that used by arbitrators today.*[129]

In many cases, religious organizations have been on the "cutting edge" of arbitration, having such procedures in place for centuries. One court referred to religious dispute resolution tribunals as "analogs to arbitration."[130]

George Washington included a clause in his will providing for the arbitration of any disputes between his heirs.[131]

Arbitration has been increasingly utilized in recent decades to handle business disputes.[132] For example, in 1944 the insurance industry set up a program for the voluntary arbitration of disputes between insurance companies.[133]

Arbitration is also frequently employed in labor disputes. The courts will seldom interfere with the determinations of arbitrators selected by employers and employees. As one court noted in 1935: "Arbitration is a favorite of the law and an award not lightly to be interfered with. Arbitrators may go wrong and yet their decision be final."[134]

National Labor Relations Board member Joseph Jenkins described arbitrators as "peacemakers" in labor disputes:

> *I call arbitrators "peacemakers" because they have it within their power to contribute more to the maintenance of good relations between conflicting forces in our society than any other group, whether public or private.*[135]

Former U.S. Supreme Court Justice Arthur Goldberg noted that both state legislatures and the federal government have passed legislation to encourage arbitration:

> *[O]ur legislative bodies have voiced their conviction that voluntary arbitration of disputes is favored and has an important role in a society which seeks the peaceful, prompt and just disposition of controversies involving our citizens.*[136]

In 1977 U.S. Supreme Court Chief Justice Warren Burger urged the wider use of arbitration. The relatively "simple and informal" arbitration procedures have made "incalculable contributions to commerce and trade and labor peace."[137]

Mediation

As previously noted, mediation does not impose a solution on the parties. Instead, it encourages the parties to negotiate and compromise:

> *The essence of mediation ... is compromise. The mediator does not make a decision. Rather, his aim is to persuade negotiators, by proposals or arguments, to come to voluntary agreement.*[138]

Francis Bacon noted the superiority of mediation to direct negotiations: "It is generally better to deal by speech than by letter; and by the mediation of a third than by a man's self."[139]

Mediation is a favored method of dispute resolution in labor negotiations. As noted by one labor authority, although the mediators have no authority to decide the disputes, "the power of persuasion can be more potent than the powers of compulsion or suppression."[140]

Mediation has been used successfully since the 1980s to resolve complex environmental disputes.[141]

Institute For Christian Conciliation

The Institute for Christian Conciliation (ICC) is a national organization providing a variety of ADR services. ICC has regional offices in 20 states. Their national office can be contacted at: 1537 Avenue D, Suite 352, Billings, MT 59102; (406) 256-1583.

ICC takes people through a voluntary three-step conflict resolution process. First, there is individual counseling to try to resolve the dispute without ADR. Second, if counseling is unsuccessful, the individuals submit the dispute to non-binding mediation. Third, if mediation is unsuccessful, the parties proceed to binding arbitration. These procedures follow the uniform guidelines of the Rules of Procedure for Christian Conciliation.

ICC encourages the use of "conciliation clauses" in contracts — providing in advance for the use of ADR rather than litigation to handle disputes. ICC has two versions of conciliation clauses. The more detailed version states:

> *The parties to this agreement are Christians and believe that the Bible commands them to make every effort to live at peace and to resolve disputes with each other in private or within the Christian church (see Matthew 18:15-20; 1 Corinthians 6:1-8). Therefore, the parties agree that any claim or dispute arising from or related to this agreement shall be settled by biblically based mediation and, if necessary, legally binding arbitration in accordance with the* **Rules of Procedure for Christian Conciliation** *of the Institute for Christian Conciliation. Judgment upon an arbitration award may be entered in any court otherwise having jurisdiction. The parties understand that these methods shall be the sole remedy for any controversy or claim arising out of this agreement and expressly waive their right to file a lawsuit in any civil court against one another for such disputes, except to enforce an arbitration decision.*

Their more concise conciliation clause states:

> *Any claim or dispute arising from or related to this agreement shall be settled by mediation and, if necessary, legally binding arbitration in accordance with the* **Rules of Procedure for Christian Conciliation** *of the Institute for Christian Conciliation. Judgment upon an arbitration*

award may be entered in any court otherwise having jurisdiction.

According to the ICC, these clauses are being used throughout the country by churches, businesses, schools, and ministries, including Christian Mutual Life Insurance Company, Baker Book House, Prison Fellowship Ministries, InterVarsity Christian Fellowship, Josh McDowell Ministries, the Association of Christian Schools International, Wycliffe Bible Translators, and the Church Loan Fund of the Orthodox Presbyterian Church.[142]

American Arbitration Association

The American Arbitration Association is a national ADR organization with chapters and arbitrators in almost every state. Their principal focus is on arbitrating business disputes.

The American Arbitration Association recommends that contracts include the following arbitration clause:

> *Any controversy or claim arising out of or relating to this contract, or the breach thereof, shall be settled by arbitration administered by the American Arbitration Association in accordance with its [applicable] rules and judgment upon the award rendered by the arbitrator may be entered in any court having jurisdiction thereof.*[143]

Churches should request this clause in their business contracts with non-church members.

Conclusion

Arbitration and mediation are practical and cost-effective ways for churches to resolve both internal disputes and business disputes. Employ these procedures whenever possible, and include arbitration or conciliation clauses in all church contracts.

Endnotes

Chapter 1

1. *Davis v. Church of Jesus Christ of Latter Day Saints*, 796 P.2d 181 (Mont. 1990).
2. *Frye v. Rumbletown Free Methodist Church*, 657 N.E.2d 745 (Ind. Ct. App. 1995).
3. *Byrd v. Arrowood*, 455 S.E.2d 672 (N.C. Ct. App. 1995).
4. *Zimmerman v. St. Peter's Catholic Church*, 622 N.E.2d 1184, 1186 (Ohio Ct. App. 1993).
5. *Bennett v. Gitzen*, 484 P.2d 811, 813 (Colo. Ct. App. 1971).
6. *Holtslander v. C.W. Whalen & Sons*, 510 N.Y.S.2d 937, aff'd as modified, 520 N.E.2d 512 (N.Y. 1988).
7. *Church of Jesus Christ of Latter Day Saints v. Superior Court*, 714 P.2d 431, 433 (Ariz. Ct. App. 1985).
8. *J. v. Victory Tabernacle Baptist Church*, 372 S.E.2d 391, 393 (Va. 1988).
9. *N.J. v. Greater Emanuel Temple Holiness*, 611 So.2d 1036, 1038 (Ala. 1992).
10. *Kluever v. Evangelical Reformed Immanuels Congregation*, 422 N.W.2d 874 (Wis. Ct. App. 1988).
11. *Crocker v. Barr*, 409 S.E.2d 368, 371 (S.C. 1991).
12. *Fisher v. Northmoon United Methodist Church*, 679 S.W.2d 305, 306 (Mo. Ct. App. 1984).
13. *Ferreira v. Strack*, 636 A.2d 682, 687 (R.I. 1994).
14. *Graf v. St. Luke's Evangelical Lutheran Church*, 625 N.E.2d 851, 855 (Ill. Ct. App. 1993).
15. *Macedonia Baptist Church v. Gibson*, 833 S.W.2d 557, 559-60 (Tex. Ct. App. 1992).
16. *Broad Street Christian Church v. Carrington*, 234 So.2d 732, 733 (Fla. Ct. App. 1970).
17. *Hambright v. First Baptist Church-Eastwood*, 638 So.2d 865 (Ala. 1994).
18. *Monaghan v. Holy Trinity Church*, 646 A.2d 1130 (N.J. Super. 1994).
19. *Weina by Patton v. Atlantic Mutual Ins. Co.*, 508 N.W.2d 67, 69 (Wis. Ct. App. 1993).
20. *Maleare v. Peachtree City Church of Christ*, 445 S.E.2d 321 (Ga. Ct. App. 1994).
21. *Williams v. First United Church of Christ*, 318 N.E.2d 562, 566 (Ohio Ct. App. 1973).

22. *Nye v. Kemp*, 646 N.E.2d 262 (Ohio Ct. App. 1994).
23. *Brillhart v. Scheier*, 758 P.2d 219 (Kan. 1988).

Chapter 2

24. *Cantwell v. State of Connecticut*, 60 S.Ct. 900, 903 (1940).
25. *Nally v. Grace Community Church of the Valley*, 763 P.2d 948, 960 (Cal. 1988).
26. *Handley v. Richards*, 518 So.2d 682 (Ala. 1987); *Moses v. Diocese*, 863 P.2d 310, 321 n. 13 (Colo. 1993); *Byrd v. Faber*, 565 N.E.2d 584 (Ohio 1991); *Schieffer v. Catholic Archdiocese*, 508 N.W.2d 907, 911 (Neb. 1993); *E.J.M. v. Archdiocese*, 622 A.2d 1388 (Pa. Super. 1993); *Baumgartner v. First Church of Christ, Scientist*, 490 N.E.2d 1319 (Ill. Ct. App. 1986); *White v. Blackburn*, 787 P.2d 1315, 1319 (Utah Ct. App. 1990); *Cherepski v. Walker*, 913 S.W.2d 761, 767 (Ark. 1996).
27. *Hertel v. Sullivan*, 633 N.E.2d 36, 39 (Ill. Ct. App. 1994).
28. A recent decision by the intermediate New Jersey appellate court may be an exception. See *F.G. v. MacDonell*, A.2d (N.J. Super. June 14, 1996). However, this case is likely to be reviewed by the New Jersey Supreme Court.
29. *Doe v. Roman Catholic Diocese*, 862 S.W.2d 338 (Mo. 1993); *Bladen v. First Presbyterian Church*, 857 P.2d 789 (Okla. 1993); *Dausch v. Ryske*, 52 F.3d 1425 (7th Cir. 1994); *Schmidt v. Bishop*, 779 F. Supp. 321, 324-25 (S.D.N.Y. 1991); *Fontaine v. Roman Catholic Church*, 625 So.2d 548 (La. Ct. App. 1993).
30. *Dausch v. Ryske*, 52 F.3d 1425, 1433 (7th Cir. 1994).
31. *Snyder v. Evangelical Orthodox Church*, 264 Cal. Rptr. 640, 644 (1989).
32. *Rosicrucian Fellowship v. Rosicrucian Nonsectarian Church*, 245 P.2d 481, 487-88 (Cal. 1952).
33. *Turner v. Unification Church*, 473 F.Supp. 367, 371-72 (D.R.I. 1978), aff'd. 602 F.2d 458 (1st Cir.); *Meroni v. Holy Spirit Ass'n. for Unification*, 506 N.Y.S.2d 174 (1986).
34. *Guinn v. Church of Christ of Collinsville*, 775 P.2d 766, 799 (Okl. 1989).
35. *Nunn v. Black*, 506 F.Supp. 444, 448 (N.D. Va. 1981), aff'd. 661 F.2d 925 (4th Cir. 1981).
36. *Paul v. Watchtower Bible & Tract Soc.*, 819 F.2d 875 (9th Cir. 1987).
37. *Bear v. Reformed Mennonite Church*, 341 A.2d 105 (Pa. 1975).
38. *Hester v. Barnett*, 723 S.W.2d 544, 559-60 (Mo. Ct. App. 1987).
39. *McAdoo v. Diaz*, 884 P.2d 1385 (Alaska 1994).
40. *Marks v. Estate of Hartgerink*, 528 N.W.2d 539, 546 (Iowa 1995).
41. See *Marks v. Estate of Hartgerink*, 528 N.W.2d 539, 546 (Iowa 1995); *Browning v. Gomez*, 332 S.W.2d 588, 591 (Tex. Ct. App. 1960); *Singleton v. Christ Servant Evangelical Lutheran Church*, 541 N.W.2d 600, 615 (Minn. Ct. App. 1996).
42. *Joiner v. Weeks*, 383 So.2d 101, 106 (La. Ct. App. 1980).
43. *Murphy v. Harty*, 393 P.2d 206, 214-16 (Or. 1964).

44. *O'Neil v. Schuckardt*, 733 P.2d 693 (Ida. 1986).
45. *Bush*, 419 P.2d 132, 137 (Wash. 1966).
46. *Molko v. Holy Spirit Ass'n.*, 762 P.2d 46, 60 (Cal. 1988).
47. *White v. Blackburn*, 787 P.2d 1315 (Utah Ct. App. 1990).
48. *Murphy v. I.S.K. Con. of New England*, 571 N.E.2d 340, 348 (Mass. 1991).

Chapter 3

49. *Jones by Jones v. Trane*, 591 N.Y.S.2d 927, 931 (1992). See also *Destefano v. Grabrian*, 763 P.2d 275, 284 (Colo. 1988); *Weaver v. Union Carbide Corp.*, 378 S.E.2d 105 (W.Va. 1984).
50. *Erickson v. Christenson*, 781 P.2d 383, 386 (Or. Ct. App. 1989).
51. *Schmidt v. Bishop*, 779 F. Supp. 321, 328 (S.D.N.Y. 1991). See also *Schieffer v. Catholic Archdiocese of Omaha*, 508 N.W.2d 907, 912 (Neb. 1993); *H.R.B. v. J.L.G.*, 913 S.W.2d 92, 98-99 (Mo. Ct. App. 1995); *Strock v. Pressnell*, 527 N.E.2d 1235, 1243-44 (Ohio 1988).
52. *Dausch v. Ryske*, 52 F.3d 1425, 1438 (7th Cir. 1994).
53. *Pritzlaff v. Archdiocese of Milwaukee*, 533 N.W.2d 780 (Wis. 1995).
54. *O'Reilly & Srasser*, 7 St. Thomas L.Rev. 31, 49-51 (1994).
55. *Moses v. Diocese of Colorado*, 863 P.2d 310, 328 (Colo. 1993).
56. *Byrd v. Faber*, 565 N.E.2d 584, 590 (Ohio 1991).
57. *Isely v. Capuchin Province*, 880 F. Supp. 1138 (E.D. Mich. 1995).
58. *Milla v. Tamayo*, 232 Ca. Rptr. 685, 690 (1986).
59. *Phillips v. Marist Society of Washington Province*, 80 F.3d 274, 277 (8th Cir. 1996).
60. *Doe v. Roman Catholic Church for the Archdiocese of New Orleans*, 615 So.2d 410, 415 (Ga. Ct. App. 1993).
61. *Lovelace v. Kechane*, 831 P.2d 624 (Okl. 1992).

Chapter 4

62. *Employment Division, Dept. of Human Resource of Oregon v. Smith*, 110 S.Ct. 1595, 1600 (1990).
63. *Serbian Eastern Orthodox Diocese v. Milivojevich*, 96 S.Ct. 2372, 2384-86 (1976).
64. *Morrow v. Hill*, 364 N.E.2d 1156, 1158 (Ohio 1977).
65. *Id.*
66. *Serbian*, 96 S.Ct. at 2382.
67. *Tibbs v. Kendrick*, 637 N.E.2d 397, 402 (Ohio Ct. App. 1994). See also *Robinson v. Davis*, 511 N.Y.S.2d 311 (1987); *Gillespie v. Elkins S. Baptist Church*, 350 S.E.2d 715 (W.Va. 1986); *Beulah Missionary Baptist Church v. Spann*, 346 N.W.2d 911 (Mich. Ct. App. 1984).
68. *Atterberry v. Smith*, 522 A.2d 683, 687 (Pa. Ct. App. 1987).
69. *Minker v. Baltimore Annual Conference of United Methodist Church*, 894 F.2d 1354, 1357 (D.C. Cir. 1990).

70. *Van Osdol v. Vogt*, 908 P.2d 1122, 1129 (Colo. 1996).
71. *Lewis v. Seventh Day Adventists Lake Region Conference*, 978 F.2d 940 (6th Cir. 1992). See also *Natal v. Christian & Missionary Alliance*, 878 F.2d 1575 (1st Cir. 1989).
72. *Scharon v. St. Luke's Episcopal Presbyterian Hospitals*, 929 F.2d 360, 363 (8th Cir. 1991).
73. *Green v. United Pentecostal Church*, 899 S.W.2d 28, 30 (Tex. Ct. App. 1995).
74. *Pierce v. Iowa-Missouri Conference of Seventh-Day Adventists*, 534 N.W.2d 425 (Iowa 1995).
75. *Fellowship Tabernacle, Inc. v. Baker*, 869 P.2d 578 (Id. Ct. App. 1994).
76. *Welter v. Seton Hall University*, 608 A.2d 206, 215-16 (N.J. 1992).
77. *Little v. Wuerl*, 929 F.2d 944, 945 (3rd Cir. 1991).
78. *Elmora Hebrew Center, Inc. v. Fishman*, 593 A.2d 725 (N.J. 1991).
79. *Rayburn v. General Conf. of Seventh Day Adventists*, 772 F.2d 1164, 1169 (4th Cir. 1985).
80. *Id.* at 1168-69.
81. *EEOC v. Southwestern Baptist Theological Seminary*, 651 F.2d 277 (5th Cir. 1981).
82. *EEOC v. Fremont Christian School*, 781 F.2d 1362, 1368-69 (9th Cir. 1986).
83. *EEOC v. Pacific Press Publishing Ass'n*, 676 F.2d 1272, 1280 (9th Cir. 1982).
84. *NLRB v. Catholic Bishop of Chicago*, 99 S.Ct. 1313, 1320 (1979).
85. *Catholic Bishop of Chicago v. National Labor Relations Board*, 559 F.2d 1112, 1124 (7th Cir. 1977).
86. *Catholic High School Ass'n. of Archdiocese of N.Y. v. Culvert*, 753 F.2d 1161, 1171 (2nd Cir. 1985).
87. *St. Luke Evangelical Lutheran Church, Inc. v. Smith*, 537 A.2d 1196 (Md. Ct. App. 1988).
88. *Maciejewski v. Breitenbeck*, 413 N.W.2d 65, 66 (Mich. Ct. App. 1987).
89. *DeMarco v. Holy Cross High School*, 4 F.3d 166, 170 (2nd Cir. 1993). See also *Weissman v. Congregation Shaare Emeth*, 38 F.3d 1038, 1044 (8th Cir. 1994); *Geary v. Visitation of the Blessed Virgin Mary Parish School*, 7 F.3d 324, 328 (3rd Cir. 1993).

Chapter 5

90. *Ward v. Jones*, 587 N.Y.S.2d 94, 97 (1992).
91. *Presbyterian Church in the United States v. Blue Hull Memorial Church*, 89 S.Ct. 601, 606 (1969).
92. *Clay v. Illinois District Council of Assemblies of God Church*, 657 N.E.2d 688, 693 (Ill. Ct. App. 1995).
93. Adams and Hanlon, *Jones v. Wolf: Church Autonomy and the Religion Clauses of the First Amendment*, 128 U. Pa.L.Rev. 1291, 1336 (1980).
94. Note, *Constitutional Law-First Amendment — The Rule of Civil Courts in Church Disputes*, 1977 Wis. L.Rev. 904, 909-13.

95. *First Presbyterian Church of Schenectady v. United Presbyterian Church of the United States*, 464 N.E.2d 454, 460 (N.Y. 1984).
96. *Jones v. Wolf*, 99 S.Ct. 3020, 3025 (1979).
97. *Id.* at 3025.
98. *Id.* at 3026.
99. *Calvary Pres. Church v. Presbytery*, 386 A.2d 357, 363 (Md. Ct. App. 1978).
100. *Church of God in Christ v. Graham*, 54 F.3d 522, 526-27 (8th Cir. 1995).
101. *Protestant Episcopal Church v. Graves*, 417 A.2d 19, 23 (N.J. 1980).
102. *Board of Incorporators of African Methodist Episcopal Church v. Mt. Olive African Methodist Episcopal Church of Fruitland, Inc.*, 672 A.2d 679, 688-95 (Md. Ct. App. 1996).
103. *Rector, Wardens and Vestrymen of Trinity-St. Michael's Parish v. Episcopal Church*, 620 A.2d 1280 (Conn. 1993).
104. *Foss v. Dykstra*, 342 N.W.2d 220, 224 (S.D. 1983).
105. *Protestant Episcopal Church v. Barker*, 171 Cal. Rptr. 541, 552 (1981).
106. *Green v. Westgate Apostolic Church*, 808 S.W.2d 547, 552 (Tex. Ct. App. 1991).
107. *Aglikin v. Kovacheff*, 516 N.E.2d 704, 709 (Ill. Ct. App. 1987).
108. *Synanon Foundation, Inc. v. California*, 100 S.Ct. 496 (1979). See also *Graffam v. Way*, 437 A.2d 627, 635 (Me. 1981).
109. *Gipson v. Brown*, 749 S.W.2d 297, 300 (Ark. 1988).
110. *Bourgeois v. Landrum*, 396 So.2d 1275, 1277-78 (La. 1981).
111. *Reid v. Gholson*, 327 S.E.2d 107, 114 (Va. 1985).
112. *Burnett v. Banks*, 279 P.2d 579 (Cal. 1955); *Willis v. Davis*, 323 S.W.2d 847 (Ky. Ct. App. 1959); *Horodeckyi v. Horodnlak*, 182 N.Y.S.2d 280 (1958); *Waters v. Hargest*, 593 S.W.2d 364 (Tex. Ct. App. 1979).
113. *Stone v. Salt Lake City*, 356 P.2d 631, 634 (Utah 1960). See also Restatement (Second) of Trusts §391.
114. *Urantia Foundation v. Maaherra*, 895 F. Supp. 1329, 1332 (D. Ariz. 1995).
115. *Bridge Pub., Inc. v. Vien*, 827 F. Supp. 629, 635 (S.D. Cal. 1993).

Chapter 6

116. See *Society of Roman Catholic Church v. Interstate Fire & Cas. Co.*, 26 F.3d 1359, 1364 (5th Cir. 1994) (archdiocese covered for negligent supervision); *Interstate Fire & Cas. Co. v. Archdiocese of Portland*, 35 F.3d 1325, 1329 (9th Cir. 1994) (same).
117. *Diocese of Winona v. Interstate Fire & Cas. Co.*, 841 F. Supp. 894, 897 (D. Minn. 1992) (no coverage for punitive damages), 858 F. Supp. 1407, 1415-19 (D. Minn. 1994) (coverage for negligent supervision), modified 916 F. Supp. 923 (D. Minn. 1995).
118. *Standard Fire Ins. Co. v. Peoples Church of Fresno*, 985 F.2d 446, 450 (9th Cir. 1993).
119. *American & Foreign Ins. Co. v. Church Schools in the Diocese of Virginia*, 645 F. Supp. 628, 633-34 (E.D. Va. 1986).

120. *All American Ins. Co. v. Burns*, 971 F.2d 438, 440-41 (10th Cir. 1992).
121. *Maryland Cas. Co. v. Huger*, 728 S.W.2d 574, 582 (Mo. Ct. App. 1987).
122. *Tichenor v. Roman Catholic Church of the Archdiocese of New Orleans*, 32 F.3d 953, 963 (5th Cir. 1994).
123. *Turner v. Church Mutual Ins. Co.*, 894 F. Supp. 191, 193-94 (E.D. Pa. 1995).
124. *Andover v. Continental Cas. Co.*, 930 F.2d 89 (1st Cir. 1989).
125. See e.g. *Essick v. Barksdale*, 882 F. Supp. 365 (D. Del. 1995).

Chapter 7

126. See *Gonzalez v. Archbishop*, 50 S.Ct. 5, 7 (1929) (appointment of chaplain left to religious authorities even though it had secondary effect on property rights).
127. *Hardwick v. First Baptist Church*, 524 A.2d 1298 (N.J. Ct. App. 1987).
128. *McAmis v. Panhandle Pipe Line Co.*, 23 L.A. 570, 574 (Kan. Ct. App. 1954).
129. Elkouri, *How Arbitration Works* at 2 (4th ed. 1985).
130. *Elmora Hebrew Center, Inc. v. Fishman*, 593 A.2d 725, 731 (N.J. 1991).
131. *AAA Arbitration News* No. 2 (1963).
132. Note, *Commercial Arbitration: Expanding the Judicial Rule*, 52 Minn. L. Rev. 1218 (1968).
133. Bernard L. Hines, *Arbitration and Mediation*, Vol. 1 at 3-5.
134. *Mueller v. Chicago & N.W. Ry.*, 259 N.W. 798, 800 (Minn. 1935).
135. Jenkins, "The Peacemakers," 47 Geo. L.J. 435, 436 (1959).
136. Goldberg, "A Supreme Court Justice Looks at Arbitration," 20 Arb. J. 13 (1965).
137. *AAA News & Views*, No. 4 (1977).
138. Elkouri, *How Arbitration Works* at 4.
139. *The Essays of Francis Bacon*, XLVII Of Negotiating (M.A. Scott 1908).
140. Simkin, *Mediation and the Dynamics of Collective Bargaining* (BNA 1971).
141. Bingham, *Resolving Environmental Disputes: A Decade of Experience*, 17 Resolve 1 (1986).
142. *Christian Conciliation Handbook* (1994).
143. American Arbitration Association, *Drafting Dispute Resolution Clauses*, at 2 (1993).

www.ingramcontent.com/pod-product-compliance
Lightning Source LLC
Chambersburg PA
CBHW071756040426
42446CB00012B/2581